PICTURE THIS!

# Winter

Karen Bryant-Mole

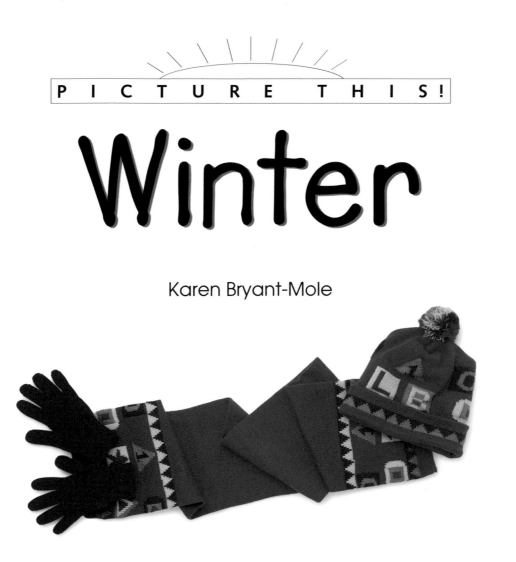

RIGBY
INTERACTIVE
LIBRARY

This edition ©1997 Reed Educational & Professional Publishing
Published by Rigby Interactive Library,
an imprint of Reed Educational & Professional Publishing,
500 Coventry Lane
Crystal Lake, IL 60014

Printed in China
01 00 99 98 97
10 9 8 7 6 5 4 3 2 1

**Library of Congress Cataloging-in-Publication Data**

Bryant-Mole, Karen.
   Winter / Karen Bryant-Mole.
      p.  cm. — (Picture this!)   Includes index.
   Summary: Text and labeled photographs identify things associated with winter.
      ISBN 1-57572-058-2 (lib. bdg.)
      1. Winter—Juvenile literature. [1. Winter.] I. Title.
      II. Series: Bryant-Mole, Karen.  Picture this!
QB637.8.B79   1997
508.2—dc21                                                        97-392
                                                                  CIP
                                                                  AC

Text designed by Jean Wheeler

**Acknowledgments**
The publisher would like to thank the following for permission to reproduce photographs.
Cephas, p. 6.(right); Mike Herringshaw/Chapel Studios, p. 19 (right); Graham Horner/Eye Ubiquitous, p. 11 (left); David Gill/Oxford Scientific Films, P. 7 (left); Arthur Butler, p.14 (left); Claude Sifelman, p. 15 (left); Chris Sharp/Positive Images, p. 6 (left); Tony Stone Images, p. 7 (left); Darrell Gulin, p.10 (left); Bob Torrez, p. 11 (right); Colin Raw, p. 11 (right); David R. Frazier, p.14 (right); J. F. Preedy, p. 15 (right); Natalie Fobes, p. 22 (left); Mike Timo, p. 22 and 23 (both right); Mark Junak, p. 23 (left); Hiroyuki Matsumoto/Zefa, p. 18 (left), p. 19 (left).

---

## Note to the Reader
Some words in this book may be new to you.
You may look them up in the glossary on page 24.

---

# Contents

# Vegetables

**Brussels sprouts**

**leeks**

**turnips**

**acorn squash**

**celery**

Some vegetables are available in winter.

# Flowers

Even in winter, there are flowers in bloom.

snowdrops

pansies

winter aconite

crocuses

# Bedtime

These things keep you cozy at bedtime.

**a hot water bottle in a cover**

a soft toy

slippers

9

# Snow

**in the forest**

Many places get snow during the winter.

**in the country**

in the park

on the road

# Clothes

These clothes will keep
you warm on a chilly day.

**gloves**

**scarf**

ski hat

# Animals

Some animals rest through
the cold winter months.

**black bear**

**dormouse**

**snow geese**

**caribou**

Some travel to
warmer places.

# Indoor Games

These games are fun to play when it's too cold to play outside.

## table games

**hand-held video game**

**jigsaw puzzle**

# Holidays

Here are some holidays that take place during the winter.

**Chinese New Year**

## Hanukkah

**Christmas**

**Mardi Gras**

These decorations could be used
to decorate a Christmas tree.

# Sports

Many people enjoy these sports during the winter.

**sledding**

*skiing*

**ice skating**

**snowboarding**

# Glossary

**bloom**  When flowers open out.
**caribou**  Wild reindeer.
**dormouse**  Small mouse that looks like a squirrel.
**Mardi Gras**  The Tuesday before Ash Wednesday, the first day of Lent. It's celebrated as a carnival in some cities.

# Index